The ABC guide of
Wireless Expense Management

©2012 Normand Cyr. All rights reserved
ISBN 978-1-105-58346-9

Preface

Are you looking for a roadmap to start your Wireless Expense Management (WEM) project? This is a must read document before you engage into crucial decision-making process. If you have already started your project you will be able to either validate or re-align some of your decisions to avoid pitfalls and traps along the road.

This book is intended to assist individuals who want to quickly learn the best approach when there's a Wireless Fleet & Expense Management project to be implemented. These recommendations are based on my years of experience partnering with wireless carriers and all the things that you may not be aware of from the beginning of your wireless relationship.

You've probably noticed by now that the Wireless Industry can be a jungle. The wireless industry is the most profitable segment of telecom with the highest and fastest penetration rate of any technology around the globe.

The corporate world can't simply cope with this fast evolving trend and starts to realize that wireless fleet management is crucial to avoid shortfall on budget. Even further, a good Wireless Expense Management project implementation can generate significant savings 25-40% according to worldwide analyst firms (Gartner, Forrester, etc…) which can translate into saving jobs for some organizations.

My expertise in this industry has clearly guided me to become a subject matter expert. My passion and profound enthusiasm entices me to share my industry secrets with you to increase efficiency in your company's wireless management. I am a firm believer in democratization of knowledge.

I invite you to join the debate by writing me your thoughts and comments which may be shared within our user community.

Hoping the following lines will inspire you to embrace your WEM project.

NORMAND CYR
ncyr@mobilemaestria.com

Chapter 1

You've got the wireless phone project, now what!

This is great! There's a new project that's been assigned to you based on your success track record on projects but you don't know much about the Wireless Industry. As well, you get the sentiment that they want to confuse you with all those plans, options and devices. Yes, the Wireless Industry is a real Kingdom of confusion! But there is hope. Over the past decade, there's been tremendous progress done in the new management practice of Wireless Fleet & Expense Management (WFEM). The US market is leading the way with multiple vendors and associations but other parts of the world such as Canada and EU are catching up quickly.

The first thing to do is to build your case with facts. You need to aggregate all possible information from your corporate wireless fleet; number of active phones, monthly cost, usage statistics, order process, service providers contact. You also need to identify if devices are under corporate liability (CL) or individual liability (IL) (see next chapter). This will make a huge difference when time comes to negotiate with the carriers. This might be difficult as a task to get a clear picture at first but find what you can. Something is better than nothing. Most likely, you'll find that some wireless carrier invoices are processed on expense reports. Although this is the worst case scenario to control cost because of lack of visibility, the finance group might be able to pull some info for you.

If you can access electronic invoices from your service providers, that is probably your best source of information. I recommend the assistance of a WEM provider to help you slice and dice all the variables, especially if you are dealing with more than one wireless carrier. The reason why? There are no standards in the industry on data output. You will need to be an expert on the industry and database management before you can even come up some meaningful reports.

Your report should be concise and based with facts and figures so it can be presented as a roadmap to upper management. Your success on this project depends on the upper management endorsement on the directions you're about to take, otherwise, you might be creating dangerous pitfalls for you along the way. Trust me on this one; you need to educate your management on WHY it is an important project for your organization.

Chapter 3 is all about bringing together the 2 essential conditions for a successful project.

This has been a fantastic journey for me as I've entered into the wireless field by chance, starting as a unsatisfied customer challenging my wireless carrier provider, and learning so much by asking all kinds of questions. If you're not 100% comfortable with the answer you've gotten to your question, ask around, and even ask other service providers as you will find that rules are sometimes different from wireless carriers. It brought me to a point that I realized there was a major gap that needed to be filled between wireless carriers and the corporate world. And this gap is all about management skills; managing a wireless fleet, managing employees requests, managing invoices, managing credits, etc., into an organized fashion which could provide efficiency and complete cost visibility.

Filling the gap required me to jump on this opportunity to start a company and create a powerful management tool (MaestriaWeb) that would help telecom administrators manage daily processes that encompass the management of a corporate wireless fleet. I've always been a firm believer that if an accountant can have their software to manage dollars and cents, then a telecom administrator deserves the same rights as telecom bills are getting uglier every day. So with this in mind, we struggled to create something that is first and foremost simple and data rich to use under a consolidated universal language that is easy to understand. Keep in mind that the wireless industry has no standard in electronic data output, therefore a universal language to read invoices needed to be set. This is the same in all countries around the globe. It is not rare to see data variations on the output from wireless carriers without any warnings. If you want to create an in-house application to manage your wireless fleet and invoices, be prepare to constantly invest time and resources to adjust from those variations. That's why the WEM industry still support managed service approach as it will be necessary until we reach a point of stability and standardization on the data output promise from wireless carriers.

So get into the action and start collecting information. This project might be the best thing that ever happened in your career. If you need assistance or guidance, don't hesitate to ask professionals in the matter. This will save you time and frustration but don't forget to have fun along the way.

CHAPTER 2

Before you start, understand the real benefits of WEM.

Too often I've seen corporations adopt a Wireless Expense Management (WEM) solution, hoping the magic will do it all. But it doesn't! Managers who want to engage in WEM need to identify what their objectives are from this initiative. Is it cost cutting, perform audit on invoice, control employees on usage? I think that the WEM market has a lot to offer, but yet is not well understood by corporations. Managers should be able to answer to the following questions before meeting with WEM vendors;

How many devices do we have under responsibility?—*we call it a wireless fleet*

Is our corporate telecom policy up-to-date?

What is our annual spending on wireless devices?

Do we have the best offer from our wireless service providers?

Centralized or decentralized billing?

Going for corporate or individual liability?

Do we have a standardized and respected procurement process?

Is expense report reimbursement the best approach to control cost?

How do we identify and control abusive usage?

Do we manage business travelers and roaming fees?

If you are able to answer those questions then the first step toward engaging with a WEM is promising. Yes there is hope and you've got the right attitude. Implementing a WEM solution (or even going with an outsourcing service) requires involvement from the organization and serious training and planning time from your schedule.

In addition to this, you will need to consider the impact of your WEM project on the IT department. Because wireless devices are proliferating and becoming more complex to manage (equipment and interface), it puts a lot of pressure on the IT help desk. The success of your WEM project will depend on your ability to discuss, plan, coordinate and share results with a group of department representatives. This will ensure stronger adoption on changes and support that will be required along the road. So roll up your sleeves and let's get started.

CHAPTER 3

IL or CL; you've got to decide which road to take!

There have been mixed opinions on the subject. Let's try to clarify things for you.

IL (Individual Liability)

This means that the wireless lines responsibility is to the employee. They are the only one that can make changes to the account profile. They are accountable for all charges, legitimate or not, and perform dispute management with the service provider if the case arise. This approach takes the responsibility away from the corporation; they don't have to manage it. However, they might be paying for it through the expense report process. I've seen customers in the past (CFO's) stating that they have a reimbursement policy in place with limited monthly allocation. This sounds great in theory but applying it to real life is really difficult, especially when it concerns sales reps. They will dispute to their manager that most of calls are for business, therefore, should be reimbursed and they are, most of the time! So where is the budget control process?

Another downside of this approach is about losing all benefits from real corporate cost saving plans. I'm talking about pooling (see our white paper on our website) voice and data. IL provides no access to <u>hidden</u> best plans from the industry. Corporations that adopt this approach have gotten half way into real WEM project. In fact, with the proliferation of smartphones with access to many mobile applications (online stores from various phone makers) forces corporations to review their budget to much higher limits…probably more than what they could have done with a well negotiated plan.

The IL approach means that you are transferring the decision making process of cost optimization to all employees. It would be unwise to believe that all employees are wireless industry experts and can make decisions with wireless carrier customer care agent to review plan assortment when the hidden agenda from a wireless carrier is to make as much profit as possible from their users. In fact, most of the time, by adding features to a plan, you only justify a fraction of the extra usage from the base plan and the residual unused feature (minutes or data) serves as an insurance to reassure the user and avoid surprises. This might be a reasonable decision for that moment, however over time you realize that these extras were not needed but most people do not go back on their plan or revise them.

In many cases, optimization reviews we have done over the years, I've seen a tremendous spread of unnecessary features assigned to wireless phone lines which translated into expensive useless cost to the organization. The point is that IL has some benefits for organization who needs less attention on the wireless fleet cost, however, like mentioned before, the proliferation of smartphone into enterprises is creating a potential massive cost explosion especially if employees are required to travel internationally. Data usage, while roaming, is extremely expensive and impossible to work out dispute management as the employee is fully responsible for the usage and cost of his mobile device.

Corporate Liability

Corporate liability engages the organization into a formal relationship with wireless carriers. Engagement to contract will include accountability to pay bills, minimum of active lines, and good usage of wireless network; clauses that are stipulated on contracts. Yes it might be intimidating but benefits surpass the contract conditions. Let me explain it.

Under corporate liability you can get individual billing (which requires a credit card credential for each user) or centralized billing. CL provides access to a broader range of plans tailored to corporations which could significantly contribute to cost reduction. Centralized billing provides additional cost saving plans that are not always offered by carriers unless they are specifically asked. I'm talking about pooling programs or by the minute plans. Since carriers are saving on invoice processing and postage, they pass along those savings to clients but this represents a fraction of all savings that are at your reach.

Optimizing a wireless fleet under CL provides more cost efficiencies as decision-making rest under account authorized individual, most likely you, the telecom admin. Therefore, from your industry expertise, you will take decisions that are relevant to the overall picture of your organization's wireless fleet. There are so many options available out there to proceed with fleet optimization that you need to focus on where cost is hurting the most. It could be long distance charges, SMS usage, roaming fees, etc…But the key lesson learned is to follow up on those change requests. Even if you have requested some changes (add or removal) on features to wireless lines, it doesn't mean that your wireless carriers are making the changes for good. Your job will be to monitor those changes and ensure that your instructions have been followed to the letter. Yes this might represent extra work but you have to understand that if your account doesn't have a dedicated customer service agent, you're exposed to human errors as you will be dealing with different individuals. Don't get me wrong here; I'm not saying that wireless carriers customer service agents are doing this on purpose. You have to understand that they are under a lot of pressure as the volume of requests coming their way have significantly increased over the past 5 years, and customer service departments are barely meeting minimum requirements on service level these days. So the trick is, if you have a significant fleet of wireless devices, then show your service provider that you are in control, you have greater chances to get a dedicated agent for your service which will release some pressure on your points of controls on change requests.

Finally, if you know what your needs are, based on real usage statistics, you will put yourself in a powerful negotiation seat, or should I say THE driver's seat. This is not a secret; carriers are blinding you with dust in the eyes by featuring options that you might not need at all. So be prepared and you'll enjoy this negotiation process.

So what is best between IL and CL? It all depends on your corporate objectives and willingness to go half way or not on your WEM project.

CHAPTER 4

Essential conditions for success factor

After more than a decade of WEM practice, the roadmap to a successful implementation of a WEM project has never been clearer to me. I've seen and read many things (good and bad) on our industry however what makes consensus is the following.

There are two essential conditions to ensure liability and success to a WEM (or TEM) project implementation, **Ownership and Endorsement**. Let me explain.

In most cases, an organization's willingness to streamline cost on wireless invoices is legitimate. They recognize the problem and wish to address it as quickly as possible. Some will rely on their wireless service provider to fix the problem....which is strange as it would be similar to giving your provider a blank cheque to solve issues that they might have no interest in solving at all. It is crucial that the organization who wants to go this way assign the project to a capable resource (internal or external) who will become the champion of the project.

Ownership on a WEM project doesn't stop at filling the blanks of provisioning and problem solving. It also includes the responsibility of budget performance, therefore invoice compliancy to guidelines and objectives. This means that the owner of a WEM project will directly impact the bottom line of an organization (hopefully positively) with actions taken to the benefit of his (her) employer. This ownership responsibility comes also with leadership liability. If you have been given this responsibility, you will have to demonstrate your leadership by showing how much it really cost your organization and what are your plans to achieve cost savings. This will contribute to your reputation as owner of the project and people will start to turn to you for advice and guidelines information. It is important that you achieve this guided by your values and ideas and by displaying your leadership skills; it will give you more confidence on your ability to meet and negotiate more aggressive contractual terms with your wireless service carriers. Don't go half-way on the project. Provide quarterly progress reports to upper management to ensure your project becomes an integral part of the company cost control process.

The second and also essential condition for a successful implementation is as I consider it, the **upper management Endorsement**. I started in a telecom admin role in the late 90's, I was faced with unexpected issues of exception to compliancy…to a point that they became the norm. If a C-level executive wanted something outside of the corporate policy, I didn't have the authority to refuse and challenge why it was not possible. Therefore, the project would start without full upper management endorsement, meaning providing the owner full leadership when it came to ensuring 100% compliancy to corporate policy.

To achieve upper management endorsement on a WEM project, it requires facts and figures. Why would a company pay for long distance communications on weekends for a corporate cell phone when employees are usually not working? What is the cost of phone replacement when an employee leaves the organization with the wireless device? What are the sanctions for abusive 411 service usage or even calling on datelines which creates charges to the organization? If you prepare your case with facts and figures, and review or even create a telecom policy according to your project guidelines to achieve set objectives, it will be much easier to obtain upper management endorsement and defend your project under a structured and robust corporate policy that will enable you with the authority you require.

You can't have a WEM project with one or the other conditions mentioned above. They go together and will clearly contribute to your success in delivering results that counts on the bottom line. If you have been assigned to a WEM project and don't feel that these two conditions are met, you might want to step back and review how you can get them in place before going full speed on deploying your plan. On my part, it's been a lesson learned that I've always passed on to my clients to make sure that they will in return be successful with their WEM project endeavor.

CHAPTER 5

Request for proposal (RFP)-the key to forbidden doors!

Ok. Now that you have some figures on your wireless fleet, you're probably questioning yourself if your incumbent wireless service provider is providing you their best plans and rates. Keep in mind that they know more than you do on your wireless fleet usage if you don't have access to an analysis tool from the WEM industry. You probably want to compare yourself with similar industry players. That's what we call Optimization Review which we perform on a regular basis to provide us with ammunition before engaging in serious discussions with wireless carriers.

You want to avoid going with and RFP process? Then you could turn into other carriers and request simple quotes. This will help you to understand if you're current plan is competitive enough for your organization. Things you should be looking at are:

- Cost of Voice plan
- Minutes included
- Cost of long distance
- Cost of 411 (directory assistance)
- Roaming cost saver programs (voice and data)
- Cost of Data plan (or option if linked on a smartphone)
- SMS cost saving programs
- Any additional cost from government regulations (911, taxes)
- Mobile to Mobile (M2M) inclusion and exclusion (incoming and outgoing calls)
- % interest on late payment fees
- Early cancellation fees

Don't forget also to ask for maps of coverage as this might be an issue for field people.

This base of knowledge will help you to understand the market dynamics and therefore be in a better position to make a decision if you're going with an RFP or not.

Let's do an RFP!

Yes I agree with you. This might be a painful process that takes time, patient and maybe external expertise to review proposal and perform simulations. But trust me, this might be the best decision you've made to anchor outstanding contractual conditions for your organization which will significantly contribute to the success of your WEM project. Depending on your organization regulations, the process might be well defined or totally up to you to make it up. Through this process, there are two conditions that should guide you along the way; INTEGRITY and OBJECTIVITY.

Integrity of your organization, you don't want to be accused of questionable relationships with vendors (favoritism). This means that if you're performing an RFP, through all that time, you should refrain yourself from going to public events as this may be perceived as favoring one supplier over another. They should all be treated equally and informed on the same basis of facts. You will get lots of respect from all invited suppliers if you respect this approach as a guideline for your RFP program. When publishing your RFP, you should allocate time for question period on the calendar and then study those answers. This will contribute to the fairness on your RFP to all.

Objectivity when it comes to analyzing answers from service providers, your decision should be based on facts and numbers if you can simulate offers based on history. Some individuals have fantastic sales ability which might influence your decision at the end. Beware! Ask for references and perform due diligence on them.

When writing your RFP, you will also need to review with your IT department any future needs or direction with technology (wi-fi networks, tablets, etc...). Your past history with wireless devices might not be your guidance for the future. Keep in mind that the Wireless Industry has revolutionized the world over the past 20 years....faster than television. And it's not over yet as the world is going more mobile than ever.

You should also provide some statistics which will help wireless carriers to provide quotes that are more focused and meaningful toward your organization needs. Statistics such as volume of airtime consumption, data, SMS, number of phone lines, smartphone, data sticks, and average minutes/data per user will greatly help the responders to your RFP.

The key is to provide information in a concise and clear way which will make it much easier to compare offers. Don't forget to create an evaluation grid for which you might want to inform service providers how each criteria will hold value on your evaluation.

Finally, if you have the ability to perform simulation, go for it or even request assistance from industry experts. This way, you will compare apples to apples along the way. As we are seeing more and more similarity in offers today (sometimes I'm wonder if there are any industry spies working on the case), you need to evaluation your decision on quantitative and qualitative facts. Don't forget that service is also an integral part of your decision process. This will be key if it means to port lines to another carrier; topic that is discussed in CHAPTER 7.

CHAPTER 6

Account consolidation – Here is why it's so important!

This must sound like a non-important issue to you. You might have dismissed it or even gone over it. Don't be fooled. Wireless carriers love to create billing accounts. The reason! It's easier for them to follow up with what is going and for some it becomes the denominator for cost saving features, a major benefit for them. Let me explain.

You probably know by now what pooling is. If not, refer to our website documentation section where you will find an in depth article on the subject. For some carriers, the way to aggregate the benefit of pooling will be done on the account level. The fewer users you have on single account, greater the chance that you will exceed it, which translate into additional cost (average chargeable usage) to your organization when you might be leaving unused minutes in other billing accounts. It's always a question of balancing demand and offer from voice and data pools. And to create more confusion, some carriers denominators are the plans – therefore you might end up with a pool for regular cell phones, another one for smartphone, another one for blackberries (cause they are treated differently) and finally another one for data sticks…A question you should be asking yourself; how many pools are you willing to manage?

My recommendation; always ask what is the denominator used on the billing for requested cost saving features. Get it in writing if you sign a contractual or commercial agreement. This way, you have an official document that stipulates what you are entitled for in your new agreement.

With the assistance of a good analysis tool from the WEM industry, you'll be able to visualize your pool consumption and monitor billing errors referring to the above. Trust me. There are plenty of them as most corporate customers don't pay enough attention to this concept of denominators. Stay on top of your wireless project and request the facts….in writing. You might be surprised on their reaction to your question.

Because of the proliferation of wireless devices in corporations, the hottest pool program you could get is referred as device agnostic. This means that voice or data are shared throughout the entire account regardless of limitations to type of devices or plans. Ask for it as it may represent a signification cost control contribution to your organization that might have strategic and aggressive mobility plan in the air.

In summary, account consolidation will do wonders for you. Not only will it guarantee you maximum savings on balancing offer and demand (voice and data) but it will simplify your life when it comes to managing your wireless fleet and invoice validation process. The KIS principal (keep it simple) applies here and don't be hesitant to implement…even if you are already in an agreement with your service providers. This action might contribute to cost saving, effortless until you get to your renegotiation date.

CHAPTER 7

Details, details, details!

Living and breathing the TEM/WEM industry for the past 10 years, I quickly realized that this business relies on data variables that are unstable, hard to predict and difficult to maintain. The TEM/WEM area has proven many times that the beast can be controlled. In fact, we noticed an evolution of TEM/WEM players when computer processors became more powerful.

I think we are all clear on the fact that success doesn't happen overnight. Savings can definitely be achieved, but industry experts, computer resources and time, must all be brought together to distinguish what is right or wrong and what is good or bad for the corporate client.

First, you have the carrier's data; such as electronic invoices. In most cases, first time access for our customers can be challenging for a number of reasons. There is no standard in the industry, the information is sometimes incomplete and a thorough analysis cannot be performed or simply because the customer has never requested the data before, therefore not produced. Many times in a year, we are all victims of unannounced changes to the data set from the wireless carriers. Most of the time, changes are represented in format of their electronic invoices which are done under good reasons I'm sure but this lack of communication puts us WEM vendors to be extremely agile in processing those changes to minimize impact on data and management tool structure. The time of our reaction is crucial to avoid database pollution on the client database. This requires excellent quality control processes if you want to survive in this industry. And this is just the beginning as new features, pricing, codes are constantly introduced which translated into more confusion for us all.

The second challenge resides within the walls of the corporate customer. I often say that the telecom admin should benefit from a TEM/WEM system, as an accountant would. We live in a data driven world. How can you optimize when you don't have a clear picture? So, coming back to the corporate customer, successful implementation of a TEM/WEM solution requires time and engagement. There is no such thing as a magic stick to solve your wireless billing problems. You have to understand the nature of the problems, find solutions to them with assistance from your wireless carrier representative, apply them and follow up cause assuming all your instructions will be followed to the dot is foolish. Keep in mind that in between your work, using or not a WEM system, and your service providers, there are humans that need to act on your requests but your needs might not be their priorities.

Customers have been coming to us over the years for the right reasons, but not getting involved in the way they should to make their project successful. Is this resistance to change or simply a hope that everything will get resolved on its own?

We were fortunate enough to work with a customer that allowed us to get involved from the beginning. Having us manage the entire RFP process and closing it with a BPO program (Business Process Outsourcing). Most importantly, we demonstrated our negotiating skills by signing one of the best deals on the market today. Trust has always been the cornerstone of our business relationship. Without trust, the results would have been somewhat promising, but not outstanding.

There are so many variables to consider that relying on expert advices become obvious. For example; a customer's specific data sets, market conditions and of course, industry knowledge. Making a TEM/WEM system work requires good quality data, time and commitment, along with seamless data flow for maintenance and data accuracy.

I sometimes tell my employees that the "Devil is in the details and we are in hell"! Let's make it easy for our customers.

CHAPTER 8

Porting a fleet; not a walk in the park.

Wireless carriers that want your business will tell you how easy it is to proceed with number portability. IT'S NOT! The number portability process was introduced in North America in the early 2000. It has been reviewed and authorized by government agency in most cases where the Wireless Industry is under regulations. The process works. The promise is usually that a cell phone line will be ported from one carrier to another one within 20 minutes to…5 days! Fortunately, it rarely takes that much time and if so, it's a matter of miscommunication on the portability request.

Where the process hurts is in the operational side of it when you have to port hundred plus lines at the same time, which is frequent in the corporate world as deployment is based on corporate objective to quickly take advantage of this new plan….and start saving. The reality is that number portability requires different actions from the authorized dealer (the cell phone distributor) to program the new device and set it up on the carrier's network. Then, the devices are shipped and it's up to the recipient to follow instruction to active the new device so that the line portability can be completed. Unfortunately, people don't read anymore. They are so excited to get their new device that they will barely notice the instructions that was shipped along….if there were any!

My recommendation to you if you're facing a portability deployment project is to perform it in phases starting with a small sample. This will allow you to set the rhythm with various players on the project and ensure 100% compliancy on your plan execution. Keep in mind that if it goes wrong, the first person to blame will be the owner on the project…you! So you have vested interest in making sure it goes smoothly.

I remember a recent portability deployment where we had every possible issue planned out and when we started with our sample group which was the upper management at head-office, the distributor accidentally programmed portability on the same day of distribution. This created issues where absent managers from the office got their cell phone line cut off, completely useless until their return to the office to activate their new device. This situation disturbed the process and created some negative perception on the carrier's ability to service the company…and have put the project owner on the spot to explain and rectify the issue before going further with deployment.

So beware of the process, the sample group and the ability of your supplier to follow your directions.

CHAPTER 9

Paying only for what's been agreed on – who's checking it!

So far so good! You've made it! You've negotiated much better contractual terms with your wireless service provider which will translate into major cost savings for your organization. Keep in mind that this is still academic until you start to materialize those cost savings, what I mean is that you still haven't seen an actual invoice reflecting the new terms. One thing you need to understand is the way billing systems work for wireless carriers. Those systems are huge billing platforms which cost a fortune to modify to meet new billing requirements. Those new requirements come from government regulations, taxations, or even competitive environment. When entering into very aggressive contractual conditions, you're exiting from the standard, therefore leaving the basic system. This is an exposure to billing mistakes and you've got to be on top of it when your first invoice arrives.

Each wireless carrier has consistently modified their billing systems over the last decade to meet new requirements which sometimes generated more billing problems than before. In the end, it is up to the client to validate their invoice for compliancy. So be ready for a rocky road until discipline kicks in. It could take up to 6 months (or more) before your wireless service providers get you a clean invoice based on your new contractual terms.

On top of this, billing mistakes create credits for you. Therefore, you will need to monitor credit returns on your account to ensure that money goes back in the bank toward your project profitability. (Not following up defeats the purpose) Refunds are hard to monitor if you don't have access to a WEM tool that support database management capabilities. You will need to validate each call charges to ensure compliancy on contractual terms, as billing mistakes mostly happen in that area. This invoice validation process is an integral part of a successful WEM project. It has to be performed monthly until 100% compliancy is met from your wireless service providers and then quarterly, as with time it will require less monitoring on your part.

When looking for a WEM tool, make sure that this function is 100% supported through automated validation process or alerts so you can extract data, document and proceed with credit claims from your suppliers. Through this experience, you will definitely see a shift of perception in your favor from providers as you keep them in line to provide accurate billing. If you don't have access to a system or even resources to perform such audit, the WEM industry provides expertise, service, advice and guidance.

CHAPTER 10

Surviving from roaming fees without casualties.

How can it be possible that for 1 hour of web-browsing which on an international business trip, charges make up for half (or even more) of the average wage corporate employee? In our practice, we have seen it all. The worst was an invoice of over $67,000 on data usage while on an international destination. Unlike the EU who took the bull by the horn and imposed some regulations to wireless carriers to alert users on pricey roaming charges, we, in North America, aren't able to benefit from such initiative. To get there, you will need to buy monitoring services which could be costly and time consuming to manage.

For most organizations, business travelers roaming fees are the worst enemy to deal with. Understanding that roaming has been abolished in Canada for more than a decade, when you leave the country, it is a different story. Before, we were exposed to roaming fees on voice only averaging from $2 to $5 per minute depending on the visited country. But with the proliferation of smartphone into companies, the exposure of increased usage cost is getting to voice, data and sms (mms) services. All together, they add up very quickly which could give you a heart attack when the bills hit your desk.

So you better be prepared to understand what you are dealing with. Make sure that you keep handy the real cost of roaming (per country/region) for those services with all your providers.

One of the best practices in the industry is actually to be more proactive and assign a roaming option on voice, data and/or sms for your business travelers. You can buy buckets of minutes, megabits or even blocks of sms from them but the trick is to know when your employees are traveling. To be in sync with the communication needs of those globetrotters, you might want to work with your dedicated travel agency (if it's the case) and have them to cc you on any travel bookings. This way, you will be able to react before any roaming fees hit the invoices and reduce communication costs by close to 80% on average.

Beware that some wireless carriers that will add features on your instructions but will leave it there until you tell them to remove it. So be attentive and specific on what you're writing on your instructions to avoid any dispute. You've got a lot to manage so no need to add more on your plate.

We've also seen recently some new roaming programs offered from the Canadian wireless carriers such as pooled roaming services on voice and data. Ask for it and this might save you additional trouble going forward.

So achieve your goal of overall cost reduction, you need to integrate a roaming fees buster program in your organization. By monitoring how much you pay each month on roaming fees, with detailed reports that generate these charges, you will be equipped to address the issue promptly and efficiently. Understanding that this might be intimidating to you digging into big data files, there are some good WEM tools out there that can help you quickly identify those charges. MaestriaWeb is one of them. By looking into call details, MaestriaWeb is able to provide instant visibility on your roaming fees with no limitation on wireless carriers.

If your program works, then you'll be able to eliminate most of roaming fees and report charges displaying exception or non-compliant usage. By going back to your travelers notice from your travel agency, you will be able to quickly spot billing anomalies that could come from employees deviating from established process or even your service provider who didn't follow your instructions. Therefore, you will be in a position to claim credits accordingly.

It is frequent in today's economy to see employees go shopping across the border and using the corporate wireless device to check on family. When this happens, it generates unjustified charges to the organization. We see this happen all the time with our customers. How should you address it? By implementing a strong telecom policy that will set rules on what is allowed and what isn't. The next chapter is all about creating a strong telecom policy which will contribute to help you achieve your objectives on your WEM project.

CHAPTER 11

Why a Telecom Policy is so important?

In your intent to provide results in cost control to your organization, you will require a guideline policy to dictate what is allowed and not. Otherwise, it will be extremely difficult for you to control something that every mobile user has access to exploit all wireless services and apps that could represent significant cost increase from an individual basis. A telecom policy might exist in your organization but probably needs to be updated with today's market offering. Keep in mind that a good policy is one that can be enforced and managed. Therefore when preparing your telecom policy, make sure it gets endorsement from upper management cause you will require the contribution of all managers to ensure 100% compliancy on your guidelines.

A good telecom policy will feature elements in two distinctive categories: **qualitative** and **quantitative** variables.

Qualitative variables will address issues such as employee departure, ownership of device and/or phone number, sick leave, maternity leave, vacation time, etc... It is variables that are hard to measure and need to be covered to avoid out-of-control cost increase.

Quantitative variables are the one you can measure on electronic billings from your wireless service providers. It could be items such as abusive usage of directory assistance, roaming fees (not authorized), forbidden number calling that generates cost to the organization (dating lines), etc. A good WEM system will help you identify those variables that are meaningful to your organization. The idea is to build a case with facts stating historical cost engaged on variables that could have been better controlled with a stronger telecom policy. If you approach upper management with these facts along with your drafted telecom policy, you will have much better chances to make it fly.

I remember one of our customers who looked into call details of past invoices. The surprise was to see that the company was spending way too much money on long distance calls over weekends while employees aren't usually at work. Even if you have something like free evening and weekend calls features, the long distance charges are not covered from these features and it can generate significant cost to your organization.

My recommendation to you is when you start your WEM project, take the time to review what is going on, monitor usage, frequent and exception requests to you, measure quantitative variables that are cost significant and then start drafting your telecom policy. You will be in much better control on what you want to address and discuss with your management. So prepare two lists along the way and write down what will be your qualitative and quantitative variables that should be represented in your document. Create a consultation team with participants from various department (HR, IT, Finance, etc..) to engage first discussion on your initial work. This way, you will be perceived as a project leader that engages the entire organization into this crucial project that you own. When you will be ready to present your project results to upper management, if you have followed the above steps, you will pave your road to a successful WEM project implementation.

CHAPTER 12

Lock or Unlock – that is the question!

Over the past 3 years, this subject of unlocking wireless devices has been brought to public space with many requests from iPhone users to get more from their device. Unlocking a wireless device means that you are no longer attached to your domestic wireless carrier when you're travelling outside of your country. Keep in mind that roaming fees contribute significantly to the bottom line of wireless carriers. With the influx of smartphones becoming a standard in wireless communication tools, roaming fees are affecting voice, data and SMS services.

When you unlock a device, it's like leaving your home base. All possibilities are now open to you. Therefore, you could request local rates by simply switching SIM cards into your device. This requires you to shop around, and probably understand the local language to make sure you're getting what you need. By doing so, you will be able to cut cost by almost 80% (voice and data) from your domestic service provider. This approach is excellent for the individual who is not afraid of experimenting with new approaches to wireless communication. The European and Asian users are much more advanced in adopting this usage pattern then North-Americans.

Unlocking a device has also some downsides. If you do this on a new device, the wireless carrier will disengage from covering the standard one year warranty on the device. So if it breaks, you will be on your own. From an individual perspective, this approach makes it less attractive unless the user is a globe-trotter. From a collective point of view, you have to consider how many repairs you could get in a year and weight the benefits of unlocking devices for those individuals who travel a lot.

There is also a SIM card resellers market that offer regional or even world SIM cards to address this issue of cost control while on business trips. My experience in this area over the past years has been very instructive. Before engaging into a long-term relationship with such suppliers, testing is crucial as SIM card numbers can be tricky in some countries. It all depends on who is providing the service. You want to avoid issues where the employee can't get a line to dial out for an important conference call. Ask who the carrier is that provides the service and what will be the priority on the calls made from SIM cards. The cheapest is not necessarily the most reliable alternative for your business travelers.

At Mobile Maestria, we've worked with many SIM card resellers over the years and found at the end that it is a marginal group of individuals who are willing to switch SIM cards on business trips. Is it a question of laziness or simply off handedness to directly participate in cost control on wireless communications?

A strategy of introducing unlocking devices into your wireless fleet has some risks attached to it. Because each organization is so different, you will have to weigh the pros and cons before going forward. You might also want to proceed with some testing before making up your mind on this. The idea is not to create more requests in the end but find easy ways to address roaming fees. It may be to renegotiate better programs with your wireless service providers that address those roaming fees. So be careful, identify every pitfall before you think about using this option.

CHAPTER 13

Dealing with upgrade program and ECF credits

As wireless devices get introduced to market at light speed these days, it creates pressure to maintain standard of devices within a corporate wireless fleet. What your service providers want from you is to renew your contract with them before the expiry date so that they keep you for another 36 months (most of the time). On top of this, you get those individuals who bring you a broken device to replace quickly. Unfortunately, the most basic phone you have on your fleet is no longer available. So you go ahead and purchase the newest device on the market, which creates a sense of exclusivity to the owner amongst his colleagues...which sometimes generates additional breakage in the same group. Trust me, I've seen it before. When sales representatives get together for regional meetings and start to discuss equipment, the rep with the newest device gets unwanted attention at the meeting. Few days after, don't be surprise to receive replacement request for broken device. It's our human nature of sometimes being envious.

So how can you manage those upgrades from a cost control approach? The idea is to be proactive with your wireless service provider by negotiating upgrade bundles. If you have a decent wireless fleet, you can request about 10% of your wireless fleet to be upgradable every year of your contractual engagement. Those upgrades can be used at your discretion and at the rhythm you want at no additional cost to acquire devices. Therefore, if you get in issues of broken devices that warranty is over, you can use the upgrade program to accommodate. This program works very well with a co-terminus engagement, meaning all devices contract start and end at the same date. Not considering upgrade programs in your negotiation is like leaving money on the table because you will be facing broken devices along the road. Replacing a smartphone is much more expensive as it's a computer after all. Do you realize that there is more technology on an iPhone then the first rocket that went to the moon? Take this upgrade program as a safety net to run your WEM project without too much disruption to your cost control strategy.

Because competition is so aggressive amongst wireless carriers, you can also include Early Cancellation Fees (ECF) credits in your mix when negotiating with your service providers. ECF is a charge when you leave the incumbent carrier before the end of your contract on device. Each carrier has its own rule on how to calculate ECF and can represents a significant amount if you consider porting your wireless fleet (partially or totally) to another service provider. It is extremely important to understand your exposure in that matter. You can request an activation report from your provider which will help you to calculate how much you would owe them if you cancelled the agreement. In most cases, when you come up to the table with an RFP, you can inform all suppliers about your ECF exposure for which you require credits to compensate. You will be surprised to see how they can response to help you maintain a healthy transition that would not affect your bottom line when starting your WEM project. Some carriers might be reluctant at first to do this but if you convince them that your business is worth the extra effort, then you could turn this into your benefit by ensuring you can compare all offers on the same base of judgment.

But the tricky part on ECF is the follow up when you requested them. You will need to be on top of it because it takes sometime 2-3 months before these get represented onto your bill. Ask what they will need as proof before you engage with ECF credit program. Again, each carrier has its own rule of operation.

Upgrades bundles and ECF credit program should be an integral part of your WEM project. You need to think on how and who will be managing them as they need to. These programs will make a signification contribution to the success of your WEM project.

CHAPTER 14

Bring your Own Device approach....

Recently, we've seen this BYOD (Bring Your Own Device) trend making its way to answer the pressure on organization not being able to react quickly enough with the consumerization of technology. In fact, it's never been so affordable to acquire a laptop or a smartphone of our choice. Today's demographic of workforce creates a vacuum of best talent to acquire. The HR department has found this BYOD as a valuable program to attract desired resources into organizations that demonstrate dynamism and adapt proactively to today's new world of technology. Combined with the cloud computing trend, the BYOD makes even more sense for an IT department. However, supporting foreign devices onto the corporate network could create additional stress to your help desk staff as they might not have the necessary knowledge to deal with various mobile OS or newest device features to adapt to your corporate infrastructure.

According to Gartner, it is now 10% of employees who use their own laptop at work and it goes up to 40% when it's about their smartphone. How are you preparing to face the BYOD trend? In the scope of your WEM project, you will need to consider this as a potential direction in the future. The best preparation is to read articles about it, consult outside colleagues that may have faced this issue. But the most important part of a BYOD program in my opinion is how your telecom policy will dictate the next steps. If you are requested to look into considering such a program, I would recommend to put together a work group that will need to identify all possible scenarios which some are already addressed in your telecom policy...if you took the time to create one.

CHAPTER 15

Now you've got the knowledge, step into the action

Now that you have read this book on my best advice is to start a WEM project, you should be well informed to become a project leader with credibility and conviction. The wireless industry is a complex environment to master. Don't be afraid to ask questions, participate in events, and build a network of resources that could contribute to your project.

Measure your results and progress.

It is crucial to measure the results and progress of your WEM project. Because you're embracing a project that could generate lots of cost savings to your organization, you need to set metrics of measurement of your project. From an in-depth review of your situation at the beginning of the project, this will serve you as a benchmark to measure your progress. One of the most common key indicators used in the industry would be the average cost per user. But if you want a clearer picture of your case, you will need to segment the data into areas that you will focus your energy on. Could be roaming fees, data overage, long distance charges, etc…

Create for yourself a dashboard to follow and monitor your progress. This tool will become your best reference to visualize your success along the way in your WEM project.

Communicate regularly with management

Communication is paramount in the success of your WEM project. If no one is aware of your performance, how will you ensure long-term stability on all the efforts you've put into implementing such project? Therefore, you need to set a communication process with your upper management that will report progress, success and even stress points that requires focus and improvement as this responsibility doesn't rely exclusively on your shoulders. Wireless device cost is the responsibility of every employee. Managers should be informed about your approved telecom policy so they can enforce it with appropriate reporting that you will supply to them on a monthly basis. A policy is making sense if you're able to measure and report deviation from it. You are responsible to perform such duties by providing management all appropriate tools (reports) so they can become your policy controllers in return. At the end, you will get to manage only the very few exceptions.

Find a WEM management tool that will answer most of your needs

WEM solution providers are active members of a dynamic community that offer different business solutions addressing corporate management needs. WEM is considered as a juvenile management practice that still revolves around innovation and business intelligence. It isn't generally adopted as a management practice but will be in the next decade. First, list your most important needs that you expect from a WEM tool. Through your evaluation, you will identify additional features that are offered from various suppliers which may be essential or nice to have functionalities to your work. Engaging into a WEM project without a management tool is like exploring a dark room not knowing what you're touching. You will need to demonstrate to your management the value of such a tool in your project which in return will translate into bigger savings for your organization. Recurrent audits and controls will ensure long-term discipline from your service providers and smarter use of wireless devices by all employees.

Report cost throughout the organization

Most of cost saving programs (such as pooling) from wireless carriers will lead you to a centralized billing, meaning you will receive only one invoice. Your challenge will be to first review and audit the invoice to identify discrepancies, proceed with credit claims if necessary and send reports to employees and managers to inform them about cost of usage of wireless devices. You don't want to fall into the open buffet perception from the users. You've got to show how much it really cost to the organization. At Mobile Maestria, we provide such functionality through an automated email feature that send out account statement to all users and managers. This process re-establishes the bridge of communication throughout the organization, a bridge that is broken by wireless carriers when you are on a centralized billing.

Review agreement, negotiate with carriers

With all the info that you've taken from this book, you can go back to the negotiation table and request a revision or even prepare for an RFP. You will need to dig out your contractual service agreement, understand all the clauses and prepare for a negotiation phase. If you're not doing it, you are simply passing by a major opportunity to cut cost from the source...the service provider. Keep in mind that the wireless industry is in perpetual movement therefore, competition creates pressure on pricing. My rule has always been, if you don't ask for it, you'll never get it! So prepare your case, and be ready to defend yourself so that next time when negotiation round is happening, you will sit in the driver seat.

Create and implement a telecom policy with controls

As I explained it in chapter 10, a Telecom Policy should be an integral part of your WEM project. This will dictate the rules on managing your wireless fleet and all the exceptions that come with it. Use this as your ammunition to prevent excessive usage that generates unnecessary or justified cost to your organization. By having a formal approach and approved direction on using wireless devices, you will be setting the boundaries of good practice in your organization. Don't forget to communicate this policy to all new employees and get the support from management level to enforce it. Otherwise, it will be very difficult for you to defend your project when costs are exploding and you have no control on how the employees are using their wireless device.

Be proactive and anticipate

After a few months, you will be more at ease with the subtleties of the wireless industry. You will quickly spot variable costs that could affect the performance of your WEM project. Become proactive on your approach. Try to anticipate what is coming up. Look for alternatives to address problems you might be facing. If you set yourself in that mindset, you can only succeed by showing real leadership and knowledge.

So, this is it for now. Good luck on your WEM project and don't hesitate to share your experience with me. If you have any questions that haven't been answered, or you were left with doubt, write to me and I'll try to help you as much as I can.

NORMAND CYR, ncyr@mobilemaestria.com

www.ingramcontent.com/pod-product-compliance
Lightning Source LLC
Chambersburg PA
CBHW021931170526
45157CB00005B/2283